MONEY Mindset: Reprogram Your Subconscious Mind for Wealth

Richard Trillion Mantey

Book Description

1) Unlock Your Financial Potential with a Transformative Mindset!

Are you ready to break free from limiting beliefs about money? In "Money Mindset: Reprogram Your Subconscious Mind for Wealth," you will embark on a journey to reshape your financial future. This practical guide combines insights from psychology and personal finance to help you:

- Understand Your Money Beliefs: Discover how your subconscious programming influences your financial decisions and overall wealth.
- Rewire Your Thinking: Learn powerful techniques to challenge and change negative beliefs that hold you back from financial success.
- Cultivate Abundance: Adopt a mindset that attracts opportunities, prosperity, and financial growth.
- Implement Practical Strategies: Apply actionable steps to set clear financial goals and create a roadmap to achieve them.

Whether you're starting your financial journey or looking to enhance your current mindset, this book provides the tools you need to create lasting change. Transform your relationship with money and open the door to a wealthier, more fulfilling life.

2) Unlock Your Financial Potential!

Are you ready to transform your relationship with money? In "Money Mindset: Reprogram Your Subconscious Mind for Wealth," discover how your beliefs about money shape your financial reality. This empowering guide reveals the subconscious patterns that hold you back and provides practical strategies to shift your mindset toward abundance.

Explore the deep-rooted beliefs that influence your financial decisions and learn how to reprogram your thoughts for lasting change. Through insightful exercises and actionable techniques, you'll cultivate a wealth mindset that attracts opportunities and prosperity.

Inside the Book, You Will Discover:

- Identifying Limiting Beliefs: Gain clarity on how past experiences shape your financial perspective.
- Proven Reprogramming Techniques: Utilize effective methods to replace negative beliefs with empowering affirmations.
- Actionable Steps for Success: Develop a clear roadmap to set and achieve your financial goals.
- Cultivating Resilience: Learn to navigate challenges and maintain a positive mindset.

Whether you seek financial freedom, career growth, or a healthier relationship with money, this book is your essential companion. Empower yourself to break free from self-imposed limits and embrace a life of abundance. Start your journey toward wealth and fulfillment today!

3)Transform Your Financial Future!

Are you tired of feeling stuck in a cycle of financial stress and limitations? Do you find yourself plagued by self-doubt and negative beliefs about money? In "Money Mindset: Reprogram Your Subconscious Mind for Wealth," you will discover the keys to unlocking your financial potential by reshaping your mindset from the inside out.

This transformative guide delves into the powerful connection between your subconscious beliefs and your financial reality. Most people don't realize that their thoughts and feelings about money can either propel them toward success or keep them trapped in a cycle of scarcity. By understanding and reprogramming these subconscious beliefs, you can create a mindset that attracts abundance and prosperity.

What You Will Learn:

- Identify Limiting Beliefs: Explore the deep-rooted beliefs that influence your financial decisions. Understand how past experiences, societal conditioning, and personal narratives contribute to a scarcity mindset.
- Reprogram Your Mind: Discover effective techniques to challenge and replace negative beliefs with empowering affirmations and positive thinking. Learn how to use visualization and meditation to reinforce a new, abundant mindset.
- Actionable Strategies for Success: Equip yourself with practical steps to set clear financial goals. From budgeting to investing, you'll find actionable advice tailored to help you take control of your financial future.
- Cultivate a Growth Mindset: Embrace resilience and learn how to navigate setbacks. Develop the ability to view challenges as opportunities for growth, ensuring that you remain motivated on your journey to financial success.

Why This Book Matters:

"Money Mindset" is not just another self-help book; it's a comprehensive roadmap for anyone looking to improve their financial situation. Whether you're just starting in your career, seeking to advance in your field, or wanting to break free from the chains of debt, this book provides the tools and insights you need to make lasting changes.

Who Should Read This Book:

This book is for anyone ready to take charge of their financial life, regardless of their current situation. Whether you're a student, a professional, an entrepreneur, or someone simply looking to improve your financial literacy, this book will empower you to shift your mindset and achieve your goals.

Take the First Step Toward Wealth:

Your relationship with money can change today. By applying the principles in "Money Mindset: Reprogram Your Subconscious Mind for Wealth," you'll learn to harness the power of your mind to create a life of abundance and fulfillment. Don't let limiting beliefs hold you back any longer. Start your journey to financial freedom now!

Dedication

To all those who dare to dream of a brighter financial future. May you find the courage to break free from limiting beliefs and the strength to embrace abundance. This book is dedicated to your journey of transformation, where every step brings you closer to the wealth and fulfillment you deserve. Believe in yourself and your potential, and know that the power to change your mindset—and your life—lies within you.

To my parents, whose unwavering support and guidance taught me the value of perseverance and belief in oneself. Your wisdom has been a guiding light on my journey. This book is dedicated to you as a testament to the lessons learned and the dreams pursued. May it inspire others to reshape their relationship with money and create a future filled with abundance.

To those who seek to transform their relationship with money and unlock their true potential. May this journey inspire you to challenge limiting beliefs, embrace abundance, and create a life of financial freedom. Your dreams are within reach—believe in yourself and take the first step toward a wealthier, more fulfilling future. This book is for you.

Table of Contents

Chapter 1: Understanding the Subconscious Mind

The Power of the Subconscious

The subconscious mind plays a pivotal role in shaping our beliefs, attitudes, and, ultimately, our outcomes in life, particularly concerning financial success. Unlike the conscious mind, which operates through logic and reasoning, the subconscious is a reservoir of emotions, memories, and deeply ingrained beliefs. It is responsible for our automatic responses and habits, often dictating how we perceive money and our ability to attract it. By understanding the power of the subconscious, individuals can begin to harness its potential to reprogram their thoughts about wealth and financial freedom.

One effective method to influence the subconscious is through conscious programming. This involves deliberately choosing thoughts and affirmations that align with financial success. By using positive affirmations, such as "I am worthy of financial abundance," individuals can replace limiting beliefs with empowering ones. Regularly repeating such affirmations can help embed these thoughts into the subconscious, leading to a shift in mindset that attracts wealth. This practice not only boosts confidence but also creates a sense of deservingness, which is crucial for achieving financial goals.

Visualization is another powerful technique for wealth attraction. By vividly imagining oneself in a state of financial abundance, individuals can create a mental picture that feels real and achievable. This practice engages the subconscious, as it cannot distinguish between real and imagined experiences. When combined with strong emotional feelings of joy and gratitude during visualization, the impact is amplified. By repeatedly visualizing financial success, individuals can train their subconscious to recognize opportunities, motivating them to take actionable steps toward achieving their dreams.

Meditation strategies can also play a significant role in overcoming financial fears that may be rooted in the subconscious. Regular meditation allows individuals to connect with their inner selves, providing a space to identify and release negative beliefs about money. Through mindfulness and focused breathing, one can create a sense of calm and clarity, which helps in reframing thoughts about wealth. This practice encourages individuals to confront their fears and replace them with a mindset of abundance, further solidifying their commitment to financial freedom.

Finally, cultivating an attitude of gratitude is essential in attracting wealth. Gratitude shifts focus from lack to abundance, reinforcing a positive mindset. By acknowledging and appreciating what one already has, individuals can open themselves up to receiving more. Incorporating daily habits and rituals, such as keeping a gratitude journal or expressing thankfulness for financial opportunities, can strengthen this mindset. Over time, these practices help to create a wealth mindset that not only attracts financial success but also enhances overall well-being and fulfillment in life.

How the Subconscious Influences Financial Behavior

The subconscious mind plays a pivotal role in shaping our financial behaviors, often operating behind the scenes and influencing decisions without our conscious awareness. It stores beliefs, experiences, and emotions related to money, which can either empower us toward financial success or hinder our progress. Understanding how the subconscious influences our financial behavior is crucial for anyone seeking to achieve financial freedom. By addressing and reprogramming the subconscious, individuals can align their financial habits with their conscious goals.

Visualizing wealth and abundance is a powerful practice that taps into the subconscious mind. When individuals engage in visualization, they create mental images of their desired financial outcomes, making them feel more attainable. This process helps to solidify beliefs in wealth and success, enabling the subconscious to accept these images as reality. The more vivid and emotionally charged the visualization, the more likely it is to penetrate the subconscious. Over time, these positive images can lead to changes in behavior, encouraging actions that align with the envisioned financial success.

Affirmations serve as another effective tool for reprogramming the subconscious. By consistently repeating positive statements about money and wealth, individuals can shift their internal dialogue and replace limiting beliefs with empowering ones. For instance, affirmations such as "I am worthy of financial abundance" or "Money flows to me effortlessly" can help dismantle the mental barriers that prevent financial growth. The key is to practice these affirmations regularly, allowing them to penetrate the subconscious and create a new narrative around wealth and prosperity.

Meditation strategies can be instrumental in overcoming financial fears that may stem from past experiences or societal conditioning. Through meditation, individuals can cultivate a sense of calm and awareness, enabling them to confront and release deep-seated anxieties related to money. This practice allows for reflection on financial beliefs and patterns, fostering a greater understanding of how these fears influence behavior. By integrating meditation into daily routines, individuals can create a safe space for healing and transformation, promoting a healthier relationship with money.

Lastly, cultivating a mindset of gratitude is essential for attracting wealth. Gratitude shifts focus from scarcity to abundance, reshaping how individuals perceive their financial circumstances. By regularly acknowledging and appreciating what one already has, the subconscious begins to attract more positive financial experiences. Incorporating daily habits and rituals centered around gratitude can reinforce this mindset, creating a fertile ground for wealth to flourish. By consistently practicing gratitude, individuals can develop a wealth mindset that not only enhances their financial behavior but also enriches their overall life experience.

Reprogramming the Subconscious for Wealth

Reprogramming the subconscious mind is a powerful approach to achieving financial success. It involves consciously altering the beliefs and attitudes that govern our financial behaviors. Many individuals are unaware that their subconscious beliefs about money can either propel them toward wealth or hold them back. By focusing on programming the subconscious with positive affirmations, visualization techniques, and daily rituals, anyone can create a mindset that attracts financial abundance. The journey begins with the understanding that our beliefs shape our reality, making it crucial to identify and transform limiting beliefs about wealth.

Visualization practices serve as a fundamental tool in reprogramming the subconscious. When we visualize our goals vividly, we create mental images that our subconscious mind begins to accept as reality. This technique involves imagining oneself in a state of financial freedom— experiencing the emotions, sights, and sounds associated with that success. Consistent practice of visualization allows individuals to align their subconscious beliefs with their conscious desires. By repeatedly reinforcing these visualizations, one can effectively encourage the subconscious to adopt a wealth-focused perspective, paving the way for opportunities and success to manifest in the material world.

Affirmations play a critical role in this reprogramming process. By using carefully crafted statements that reflect financial abundance, individuals can counteract negative beliefs about money. Affirmations should be positive, present tense, and emotionally resonant to be effective. For example, affirming statements like "I am a magnet for wealth" or "Money flows to me effortlessly" can create a decisive shift in mindset. Regularly repeating these affirmations strengthens the neural pathways associated with wealth, allowing the subconscious to embrace these new beliefs and act accordingly in financial matters. The consistent practice of affirmations not only reprograms the mind but also instills a sense of confidence and empowerment regarding one's economic situation.

Meditation strategies can further enhance the reprogramming of the subconscious by addressing and overcoming financial fears. Through meditation, individuals can create a space for reflection and self-awareness, allowing them to confront and release limiting beliefs related to money. By focusing on breathing and centering the mind, one can visualize financial fears dissolving and being replaced with feelings of security and abundance. This practice not only calms the mind but also reinforces a positive mindset, encouraging individuals to embrace new financial possibilities. Regular meditation can lead to profound shifts in perspective, enabling a more constructive relationship with money.

Gratitude plays a pivotal role in attracting wealth and fostering a mindset of abundance. By cultivating an attitude of gratitude, individuals shift their focus from scarcity to appreciation. This shift not only enhances overall well-being but also aligns the subconscious with the frequency of abundance. Practicing gratitude daily—whether through journaling or simply reflecting on what one is thankful for—can amplify feelings of wealth already present in one's life. Establishing a wealth mindset requires daily habits and rituals that reinforce the belief in abundance, creating a sustainable foundation for financial success. Through consistent practice, individuals can transform their subconscious programming and embrace a life of financial freedom.

Chapter 2: The Role of the Conscious Mind

Distinguishing Between Conscious and Subconscious

Understanding the distinction between the conscious and subconscious mind is crucial for anyone seeking financial success. The conscious mind is the part of our mental processing that involves active thinking, decision-making, and reasoning. It is where we formulate plans, set goals, and analyze our circumstances. This part of the mind is often engaged when we are awake and alert, allowing us to think critically about our financial situations, assess opportunities, and make informed choices. Recognizing its role is the first step in harnessing its power to influence our subconscious programming.

In contrast, the subconscious mind operates beneath the surface of our awareness. It is responsible for storing memories, habits, beliefs, and emotional responses, influencing our behavior in ways we may not consciously recognize. This aspect of our mind plays a significant role in shaping our financial reality through ingrained beliefs about money, wealth, and self-worth. For instance, if someone has a deep-seated belief that they do not deserve wealth, that belief can sabotage their conscious efforts to achieve financial success. Understanding this dynamic allows individuals to identify and address limiting beliefs that may be holding them back.

To effectively reprogram the subconscious mind for financial freedom, one must leverage the conscious mind's capabilities. Visualization practices serve as a powerful tool in this process. By vividly picturing oneself achieving financial goals, the conscious mind can create a blueprint that the subconscious can begin to adopt. This involves not only seeing the desired outcome but also feeling the emotions associated with that success. When the subconscious begins to align with these visualized scenarios, it can pave the way for actions that lead to real financial changes.

Affirmations are another valuable strategy for influencing the subconscious mind. Positive affirmations related to wealth can help to overwrite negative beliefs and create a new narrative around money. Repeating affirmations daily allows individuals to consciously affirm their worthiness of financial abundance, gradually shifting the subconscious mind toward a more prosperous mindset. This practice, when combined with visualization, can enhance the effectiveness of both techniques, reinforcing the belief that financial success is achievable.

Meditation and gratitude practices further support this journey towards financial prosperity. Meditation helps quiet the mind, allowing individuals to confront and overcome financial fears that may reside in the subconscious. By creating a space for reflection, meditation can reveal limiting beliefs and facilitate their release. Meanwhile, cultivating gratitude shifts focus from scarcity to abundance, reinforcing a mindset that attracts wealth. Daily habits and rituals that incorporate these strategies can create a strong foundation for developing a wealth mindset, ultimately leading to the financial freedom that many seek.

The Process of Reprogramming

The process of reprogramming your subconscious mind is a transformative journey that begins with the conscious decision to change your financial beliefs and behaviors. This involves recognizing the limiting beliefs you may hold about money, such as feelings of unworthiness or fear of failure. These beliefs often stem from past experiences and societal conditioning. By becoming aware of these negative thought patterns, you can start to consciously challenge and replace them with empowering beliefs that support your financial goals. This initial step is crucial, as it sets the foundation for the reprogramming process.

Visualization practices play a significant role in this reprogramming process. Visualization involves creating vivid mental images of your desired financial outcomes, such as achieving a specific income level or owning a dream home. This technique taps into the power of the subconscious mind, as it cannot distinguish between real and imagined experiences. By regularly visualizing your financial goals, you reinforce the belief that these outcomes are not only achievable but also inevitable. Incorporating this practice into your daily routine can help you maintain focus and motivation as you work toward financial freedom. You can do all these exercises for 34 days or more. Usually, it takes 21 days to program your subconscious mind. The best time to do this exercise is before you go to bed at night or first thing in the morning when you wake up. Do it over and over for 9 minutes before bed and first thing in the morning when you wake up.

Affirmations serve as another powerful tool for subconscious programming related to money. These positive statements, when repeated consistently, can rewire your brain to adopt a wealth-oriented mindset. Crafting affirmations that resonate with your aspirations is essential. For instance, saying, I am so happy and grateful now that "I am worthy of financial abundance" or "Money flows to me effortlessly" can create a shift in your perception of wealth. The key is to repeat these affirmations with conviction and emotion, allowing them to penetrate your subconscious. Over time, this practice helps to replace negative beliefs with positive affirmations that align with your financial aspirations. Repeat this affirmation and visualization for 9 minutes, 34 days straight, before you go to bed at night and first thing in the morning when you get up.

Meditation strategies can also be effective in overcoming financial fears that may hinder your progress. Engaging in regular meditation allows you to quiet the mind and connect with your inner self. This practice fosters a sense of calm and clarity, enabling you to confront and release fears related to money. By creating a safe mental space, you can explore your financial anxieties without judgment. As you consistently engage in meditation, you cultivate resilience and a deeper understanding of your financial mindset, empowering you to move forward with confidence.

Finally, cultivating a gratitude practice is essential for attracting wealth and abundance. Gratitude shifts your focus from scarcity to appreciation, allowing you to recognize and celebrate the financial blessings you already possess. This shift in perspective can significantly enhance your overall mindset. By incorporating gratitude into your daily habits and rituals, such as maintaining a gratitude journal or expressing thanks for small financial wins, you create a positive feedback loop that attracts more abundance into your life. As you reinforce a wealth mindset through these daily practices, you align your subconscious with the energy of prosperity, paving the way for lasting financial success.

Techniques for Engaging the Conscious Mind

Engaging the conscious mind is a pivotal step in the journey toward reprogramming the subconscious for financial success. The conscious mind serves as the gatekeeper of thoughts and beliefs, and by harnessing its power, individuals can instigate transformative changes in their financial outlook. Techniques such as visualization, affirmations, and meditation provide robust frameworks for this engagement, allowing one to cultivate a mindset that attracts wealth and abundance. Understanding how to employ these techniques effectively can lead to a profound shift in one's financial reality.

Visualization practices are among the most effective techniques for engaging the conscious mind to attract wealth. This involves vividly imagining the financial goals one wishes to achieve, whether it's a specific income level, a successful business, or a lifestyle of abundance. Creating a detailed mental picture not only clarifies goals but also emotionally connects individuals to their desires. Visualizing success regularly reinforces the belief that achieving financial freedom is possible. Utilizing tools such as vision boards or guided imagery can enhance this practice, making the envisioned outcomes feel more tangible and achievable.

Affirmations serve as another powerful tool for programming the subconscious mind through the conscious mind. By repeating positive statements related to wealth and abundance, individuals can counteract negative beliefs that may have been ingrained over time. For example, affirmations such as "I am worthy of financial success" or "Money flows easily into my life" can help reshape one's belief system. Consistency is vital; integrating affirmations into daily routines, such as during morning rituals or before sleep, amplifies their effectiveness. Over time, these affirmations can help dismantle limiting beliefs and replace them with empowering truths. Repeat this affirmation before you go to bed and right when you wake up in the morning. Repeat it over and over for 34 days to reprogram your subconscious mind. There are many affirmations that you can you. Here is an example - I am so happy, grateful, and thankful now that already, day by day, night by night, an unlimited abundance of great fortune and wealth, of cash, of money flows easily into my life. I am very grateful and thankful. Here is another example - I am so happy, grateful, and thankful now that every single second of every minute, every single second of every hour, every single second of every day, I am worthy of financial success. Money flows easily into my life from unlimited sources, and I am very grateful and thankful.

Meditation strategies can also play a significant role in overcoming financial fears, which often reside within the subconscious. By engaging in regular meditation, individuals can create a space for introspection, allowing them to identify and confront underlying anxieties related to money. Techniques such as guided meditations focused on financial abundance or mindfulness practices centered on gratitude can foster a sense of peace and clarity. This mindful engagement with one's fears not only alleviates stress but also opens the door to a more expansive mindset, enabling individuals to embrace opportunities for financial growth.

Gratitude is a cornerstone in attracting wealth, as it shifts focus from scarcity to abundance. Cultivating a gratitude practice helps individuals recognize and appreciate what they already have, thereby creating a positive feedback loop that invites further abundance into their lives. Simple rituals, such as keeping a gratitude journal or regularly expressing appreciation for financial blessings, can significantly enhance one's wealth mindset. By consistently focusing on gratitude, individuals can reprogram their subconscious to expect and attract more wealth, reinforcing the belief that they are deserving of financial success.

Chapter 3: Visualization Practices for Wealth Attraction

The Science Behind Visualization

Visualization is a powerful psychological tool that leverages the mind's ability to create mental images, fostering a positive and focused mindset. This technique operates on the premise that the subconscious mind does not differentiate between real and imagined experiences. When individuals visualize their financial goals, they create a mental framework that can guide their actions and decisions toward achieving those objectives. By consistently imagining success, wealth, and abundance, individuals can program their subconscious minds to recognize opportunities and take proactive steps toward financial freedom.

The science behind visualization is rooted in cognitive psychology and neuroscience. Studies have shown that when people visualize themselves accomplishing a task, the brain activates similar neural pathways as those used when actually performing the task. This phenomenon suggests that visualization not only enhances motivation but also improves performance by preparing the brain for real-life challenges. For instance, athletes often use visualization techniques to enhance their performance, and this principle can be applied to financial success. By vividly imagining their desired financial outcomes, individuals can strengthen their belief in their ability to achieve those goals.

In conjunction with visualization, affirmations serve as a crucial component in reprogramming the subconscious mind. Affirmations are positive statements that reinforce one's self-worth and capabilities, particularly concerning financial matters. When coupled with visualization practices, affirmations amplify their effectiveness by embedding these beliefs deeper into the subconscious. For example, repeating affirmations such as "I am worthy of financial abundance" while visualizing oneself living a prosperous life can create a powerful synergy that promotes a wealth mindset. This dual approach can help dismantle limiting beliefs and foster a sense of empowerment regarding financial matters.

Meditation strategies also play a vital role in overcoming financial fears and anxieties. Engaging in regular meditation allows individuals to cultivate mindfulness, which can help them identify and address negative thought patterns related to money. By incorporating visualization into meditation practices, individuals can create a serene mental space where they can envision their financial goals without distractions. This practice not only alleviates stress but also reinforces a positive outlook on wealth. As individuals become more comfortable with their financial aspirations, they can develop resilience against fear and doubt, paving the way for a more abundant mindset.

Lastly, gratitude is an essential element in attracting wealth and fostering a favorable financial environment. By regularly practicing gratitude, individuals can shift their focus from scarcity to abundance. This shift in perspective can enhance the effectiveness of visualization and affirmations, as it fosters a deep appreciation for what one currently possesses and the potential for future growth. Developing daily habits and rituals centered around gratitude, visualization, and affirmations can create a powerful framework for cultivating a wealth mindset. By consciously engaging in practices that align with their financial goals, individuals can make a sustainable path toward financial success and abundance.

Crafting Effective Visualization Techniques

Crafting effective visualization techniques is an essential aspect of programming the subconscious mind for financial success. Visualization serves as a powerful tool that bridges the gap between one's current financial reality and the desired state of abundance. To effectively harness this technique, it is essential to create clear, detailed mental images that resonate with the emotions tied to financial prosperity. Begin by identifying specific financial goals, such as saving a certain amount, investing wisely, or achieving a debt-free status. The clearer the vision, the more tangible it becomes, allowing the subconscious to align with these aspirations, desires, or aims.

Incorporating affirmations into visualization practices enhances their effectiveness. Affirmations are positive statements that reinforce one's belief in their financial capabilities and potential. When combined with visualization, these affirmations should be spoken aloud during the visualization process. For instance, while picturing oneself enjoying financial freedom, repeating affirmations like "I am worthy of abundance" or "Wealth flows effortlessly into my life" can solidify the desired outcome in mind. This repetition helps program the subconscious, replacing limiting beliefs with a more empowering mindset that supports financial success.

Meditation can further amplify the power of visualization. Setting aside time to meditate allows for a focused and relaxed state of mind, conducive to compelling imagery. During meditation, individuals can visualize their financial goals while releasing fears or anxieties associated with money. This practice not only reduces stress but also creates a mental space where positive financial outcomes can be envisioned without distraction. By repeatedly engaging in this meditative visualization, individuals reinforce their commitment to achieving financial freedom, further embedding these positive images within their subconscious.

Gratitude plays a significant role in the visualization process as well. Cultivating a sense of appreciation for current financial circumstances, no matter how modest helps shift the focus from scarcity to abundance. Incorporating gratitude into visualization practices can be done by taking a moment to acknowledge and visualize the blessings already present in one's life. This mindset fosters a deeper connection to the feelings of wealth, making it easier to attract more prosperity. By expressing gratitude, individuals not only enhance their visualization techniques but also open themselves up to receiving greater abundance.

Finally, creating a wealth mindset through daily habits and rituals reinforces the efficacy of visualization techniques. Establishing routines that incorporate visualization, affirmations, and gratitude can lead to lasting changes in one's financial outlook. These rituals could include morning visualizations of financial goals, daily affirmations, or evening reflections on gratitude related to money. By consistently practicing these techniques, individuals create a proactive mindset that continually draws in financial prosperity. Over time, these habits become ingrained, allowing the subconscious to work harmoniously towards achieving financial success.

Daily Visualization Routines for Financial Success

Daily visualization routines can play an essential role in reprogramming your subconscious mind for financial success. Visualization is more than just daydreaming; it is a structured practice that engages your conscious mind to shape your beliefs and expectations about wealth. By dedicating time each day to visualize your financial goals, you create a mental blueprint that the subconscious can latch onto, enhancing your ability to recognize and seize opportunities. This routine can be tailored to fit your specific aspirations, dreams, or aims, whether it's achieving a certain income level, owning property, or starting a successful business.

To implement an effective visualization routine, begin by setting a clear intention. Define what financial success looks like for you. Then, find a quiet space where you can sit comfortably without distractions. Close your eyes, take a few deep breaths, and begin to picture yourself in a scenario where you have already achieved your financial goals.

Engage all your senses: visualize the environment, hear the sounds and friends and family congregating with you, and feel the emotions associated with your success. This immersive experience helps your subconscious mind internalize these images, making them feel more attainable.

Incorporating affirmations into your visualization practice amplifies its effectiveness. Affirmations are positive statements that challenge and replace negative beliefs about money. As you visualize, repeat affirmations that resonate with your financial aspirations, such as "I am worthy of financial abundance" or "Opportunities for wealth flow to me effortlessly." Combining affirmations with visualization reinforces the neural pathways in your brain related to wealth and success, making it easier for you to act in ways that align with these beliefs.

Meditation can also be a valuable addition to your daily routine. By taking a few minutes each day to meditate, you can cultivate a calm and focused mindset that reduces financial fears and anxieties. During meditation, allow thoughts about financial stress to surface without judgment, and then visualize releasing these thoughts, replacing them with images of financial stability and abundance. This practice not only alleviates fear but also fosters a sense of peace that is conducive to attracting wealth.

Finally, integrating gratitude into your daily visualization routine enhances your ability to attract financial success. Cultivating gratitude shifts your focus from scarcity to abundance, allowing you to appreciate what you already have. Begin or end your visualization practice by listing things you are grateful for, especially those related to your financial journey. This simple yet powerful act opens the door to greater abundance, reinforcing a wealth mindset and inviting more opportunities into your life. By consistently practicing these visualization routines, you empower your subconscious to align with your financial goals, paving the way for lasting financial freedom.

Chapter 4: Affirmations for Subconscious Programming

Understanding Affirmations

Understanding affirmations is crucial for anyone seeking to reprogram their subconscious mind for financial success. At their core, affirmations are positive statements that help to challenge and overcome self-sabotaging thoughts. By repeating these statements regularly, individuals can gradually change their thought patterns and beliefs about money. This shift is important in the journey toward financial freedom, as it allows one to align their conscious desires with their subconscious beliefs. The power of affirmations lies in their ability to influence the subconscious mind, the part of the brain that drives behavior and decision-making, often without conscious awareness.

Utilizing affirmations effectively requires a clear understanding of both the conscious and subconscious minds. The conscious mind is responsible for logic and reasoning, while the subconscious mind is where emotions, habits, and automatic responses reside. To achieve financial success, it is essential to create affirmations that resonate positively with the subconscious. This means using language that is not only affirmative but also emotionally charged, making the statements feel real and achievable. When individuals affirm their financial goals with conviction, they begin to rewire their subconscious, fostering a mindset that welcomes wealth and abundance. You can use the affirmation example I gave you on the previous page, or you can use this affirmation TEMPLATE and make it your own. This is the template. I am so happy, grateful, and thankful that I am already (whatever want to put here an example of what you can put in here #1 wealthy and rich, #2 a millionaire, #3 a billionaire, whatever you want to put here), and I am very grateful and thankful. MAKE SURE you repeat this affirmation 9 minutes for 34 days straight before you go to bed and right after you get up in the morning

Visualization practices complement affirmations and enhance their effectiveness. When one visualizes their financial goals while reciting affirmations, they create a powerful mental image that the subconscious can latch onto. This combination of seeing and affirming can significantly increase motivation and clarify one's desires. For instance, envisioning oneself living a life of abundance while repeating affirmations about financial prosperity can help solidify the belief that such a life is attainable. Over time, this practice can transform unclear dreams into concrete goals, making the pursuit of financial freedom feel more achievable.

Meditation strategies can also play a crucial role in overcoming financial fears and reinforcing the positive beliefs established through affirmations. By engaging in regular meditation, individuals can cultivate a sense of calm and clarity, allowing them to confront and release limiting beliefs about money. During meditation, one can reflect on their affirmations, allowing them to sink deeper into the subconscious. This practice not only helps in alleviating anxiety surrounding finances but also reinforces a positive mindset, paving the way for better financial decisions and opportunities.

Finally, gratitude is a powerful tool in the realm of affirmations and wealth attraction. By focusing on what one already has and expressing gratitude for those financial blessings, individuals can shift their mindset from scarcity to abundance. This shift enhances the effectiveness of affirmations by creating a more receptive mental environment. Daily habits and rituals that incorporate affirmations and gratitude can significantly contribute to developing a wealth mindset. By consistently practicing these principles, individuals lay the groundwork for lasting financial success, empowering them to attract wealth and create the life they desire.

Creating Powerful Money Affirmations

Creating powerful money affirmations is a transformative step toward achieving financial freedom. At their core, affirmations are positive statements that help to challenge and overcome self-sabotaging thoughts. When crafted thoughtfully, money affirmations can reprogram the subconscious mind to embrace a wealth mindset. This process begins with understanding the beliefs that currently govern your financial situation. By identifying and addressing these limiting beliefs, you can create affirmations that resonate deeply with your aspirations for financial success.

To create effective money affirmations, start by using present-tense language that reflects your desired state of being. For instance, instead of saying, "I will be wealthy," shift to "I am abundant and attract wealth effortlessly." This subtle change in phrasing signals to your subconscious that the desired state is already a part of your reality. Be specific about the outcomes you wish to achieve. Rather than generic phrases, tailor your affirmations to resonate with your personal financial goals, such as "I manage my finances wisely and effortlessly" or "Money flows to me from multiple sources." you can also use the examples I gave you previously.

Visualization is an essential companion to affirmations. As you recite your money affirmations, visualize yourself living the life you desire. Imagine the feelings of joy, security, and freedom that come with financial abundance. This mental imagery reinforces the affirmations, making them more impactful. You can enhance your visualization practice by creating a vision board that includes images and words representing your financial goals. Regularly engaging in this practice will strengthen your belief in the affirmations and keep your subconscious focused on attracting wealth.

Incorporating meditation into your daily routine can significantly amplify the effects of your money affirmations. Meditation helps to quiet the mind, allowing you to connect with your inner self and release any financial fears that may be holding you back. During meditation, you can repeat your affirmations, focusing on the emotions they evoke. This deeper connection helps solidify your new beliefs and can dissolve any lingering doubts or fears about money. By establishing a consistent meditation practice, you create a sacred space for growth and abundance in your life.

Finally, gratitude plays a vital role in the process of attracting wealth. Cultivating a habit of gratitude shifts your mindset from scarcity to abundance. When you regularly express gratitude for the money you currently have, no matter the amount, you send a powerful message to your subconscious that you are open to receiving even more. Integrating gratitude into your daily affirmations can enhance their effectiveness. Phrases like "I am grateful for the wealth that surrounds me" or "I appreciate the financial opportunities that come my way" can create a positive feedback loop that attracts further abundance. By establishing daily habits and rituals that include affirmations, visualization, meditation, and gratitude, you can create a robust framework for achieving financial success.

Incorporating Affirmations into Daily Life

Incorporating affirmations into daily life is a powerful strategy for reprogramming your subconscious mind to align with your financial goals. Affirmations are positive statements that challenge and overcome self-sabotaging thoughts. By consistently repeating affirmations related to financial success, such as "I am worthy of wealth" or "Money flows to me effortlessly," you begin to shift your mindset. This shift is crucial because the subconscious mind absorbs these affirmations, which can lead to more constructive behaviors and beliefs around money. The key is to make affirmations a regular part of your daily routine, allowing them to penetrate your subconscious and replace limiting beliefs with empowering ones.

To effectively incorporate affirmations, start by establishing a specific time for practice each day. This could be in the morning, as you prepare for the day, or at night, just before sleep. During this time, focus on your affirmations with intention and emotion. Visualize the outcomes you desire while repeating each statement. For instance, while saying, "I attract financial opportunities," picture yourself engaging in activities that lead to those opportunities. This visualization reinforces the affirmations and helps solidify the connection between your conscious desires and subconscious acceptance.

Another effective method is to create visual reminders of your affirmations. Writing them down and placing them where you will see them regularly, such as on your bathroom mirror or workspace, serves as a constant reminder of your goals. These visual cues reinforce your commitment to your affirmations and keep your financial aspirations at the forefront of your mind. Additionally, consider using technology to your advantage. Recording your affirmations and listening to them during your daily commute or while exercising can help reinforce these messages even further, making them a seamless part of your routine.

In addition to repetition and visualization, integrating gratitude into your affirmation practice can enhance its effectiveness. Expressing gratitude for what you already have creates a positive mindset and opens you up to receiving more. For example, before reciting your affirmations, take a moment to acknowledge the financial blessings you currently possess, no matter how small. This practice not only cultivates a sense of abundance but also aligns your energy with the vibrations of wealth, making it easier to attract financial opportunities.

Finally, pairing your affirmations with meditation can deepen your practice and help you overcome financial fears. Spend a few moments in silence, focusing on your breath, and allow your mind to settle. As you meditate, introduce your affirmations into your thoughts. This combination not only calms the mind but also creates a fertile space for new beliefs to take root. Over time, this practice can shift your perspective on money, reduce anxiety associated with financial issues, and foster a wealth mindset that attracts financial success. By consistently incorporating affirmations into your daily life, you create a powerful foundation for achieving your financial goals.

Chapter 5: Meditation Strategies for Overcoming Financial Fears

The Impact of Fear on Financial Success

Fear plays a significant role in shaping an individual's financial trajectory. When people experience fear related to money, it often manifests as anxiety about financial instability, fear of failure, or even fear of success. These emotions can lead to self-sabotaging behaviors, preventing individuals from taking necessary risks or pursuing opportunities that could enhance their financial situation. Understanding how fear operates in our minds is crucial for reprogramming our subconscious to align with our financial goals.

To effectively combat fear, it is essential to recognize its root causes. Many fears surrounding finances stem from past experiences, societal conditioning, or limiting beliefs that have been ingrained over time. By identifying these fears, individuals can begin to challenge and reformulate the thoughts associated with them. This process encourages the use of visualization practices, where individuals imagine themselves overcoming these fears and achieving financial success. Visualization not only creates a mental image of success but also reinforces confidence and reduces the emotional grip of fear.

Affirmations serve as a powerful tool in this reprogramming process. Positive affirmations related to financial success can counteract the negative thought patterns that fear creates.

By repeating affirmations that emphasize abundance, competence, and financial freedom, individuals can start to reshape their subconscious beliefs. This practice, when combined with consistent meditation strategies to address and release financial fears, can create a profound shift in one's mindset. Meditation helps cultivate a sense of calm and clarity, allowing individuals to observe their concerns without judgment and gradually diminish their power.

Gratitude also plays a pivotal role in attracting wealth and mitigating fear. By focusing on what they already have, individuals can shift their mindset from scarcity to abundance. This practice not only fosters a positive outlook but also reinforces the belief that financial resources are available and attainable. Incorporating gratitude into daily rituals, such as maintaining a gratitude journal or expressing appreciation for financial gains—no matter how small—can create a more abundant mindset. This shift in perspective can significantly decrease fear and encourage proactive financial behaviors.

Finally, creating daily habits and rituals that promote a wealth mindset is essential in overcoming the paralyzing effects of fear. These habits can include setting clear financial goals, educating oneself about finances, and actively seeking out opportunities for growth. By consciously choosing to engage in behaviors that support wealth creation, individuals can gradually diminish the influence of fear on their financial decisions. This proactive approach not only enhances financial literacy but also empowers individuals to take control of their financial destinies, ultimately leading to greater success and fulfillment.

Guided Meditations for Financial Confidence

Guided meditations serve as a powerful tool for cultivating financial confidence by reprogramming the subconscious mind. By engaging in these structured sessions, individuals can shift their beliefs about money and abundance. This process often involves visualizing financial success, which activates the brain's neural pathways associated with wealth attraction. Through repetition and focused intention, guided meditations facilitate a deeper understanding of one's financial aspirations, leading to a more confident approach to wealth creation.

Visualization practices play a critical role in guided meditations aimed at financial confidence. During these sessions, individuals are encouraged to vividly imagine their financial goals, such as achieving a specific income level or living a lifestyle of abundance. This not only helps clarify what financial success looks like but also aligns the subconscious mind with these aspirations. The more detailed and emotionally charged the visualization, the more effective it becomes in influencing behavior and decision-making, ultimately guiding individuals toward opportunities that support their financial objectives.

Affirmations are another essential component of guided meditations that reinforce positive beliefs about money. Phrases such as "I attract wealth effortlessly" or "I am worthy of financial success" can be integrated into meditation sessions to help overwrite limiting beliefs. Repeating these affirmations during meditation allows individuals to internalize these empowering statements, creating a strong foundation for a wealth-oriented mindset. Over time, this consistent practice fosters an attitude of abundance, encouraging individuals to take proactive steps toward achieving their financial goals.

Meditation strategies can also be instrumental in overcoming financial fears. Many individuals harbor deep-seated anxieties about money, often rooted in past experiences or cultural conditioning. Guided meditations can address these fears by creating a safe mental space where individuals can confront and release their anxieties. Techniques may include deep breathing, mindfulness, and self-compassion exercises that help individuals process their feelings about money. As they work through these emotions, they can replace fear with confidence, enabling them to approach financial decisions with clarity and calm.

Finally, cultivating gratitude through guided meditation is a transformative practice that significantly enhances one's ability to attract wealth. By expressing gratitude for current financial blessings, individuals shift their focus from scarcity to abundance. This mindset opens the door to greater financial opportunities, as gratitude cultivates a positive vibration that resonates with the energy of wealth. Incorporating daily habits and rituals centered on gratitude into financial meditation practices solidifies this mindset, reinforcing the belief that one is deserving of both current and future financial success.

Building a Meditation Practice for Wealth

Building a meditation practice for wealth begins with understanding the profound connection between the mind and financial success. Meditation allows individuals to quiet the noise of daily life, create mental clarity, and foster a deep sense of awareness. This awareness is crucial for recognizing and transforming limiting beliefs about money that may be embedded in the subconscious. By integrating meditation into your daily routine, you can set the foundation for a wealth mindset that attracts financial opportunities and abundance.

To effectively build this practice, start by establishing a dedicated time and space for meditation. This environment should be comfortable and free from distractions, allowing you to fully immerse yourself in the experience. Begin with short sessions, gradually increasing the duration as you become more comfortable. Utilize visualization techniques during these sessions by picturing financial abundance in your life. Imagine what it feels like to achieve your financial goals, engaging all your senses to create a vivid mental image that your subconscious can latch onto.

Affirmations play a vital role in programming your subconscious mind for wealth. Incorporate positive affirmations related to money into your meditation practice. Phrases like "I am worthy of financial abundance" or "Money flows effortlessly into my life" can be repeated during your sessions to reinforce a positive mindset. Consistent repetition of these affirmations helps dismantle negative beliefs about money and replaces them with empowering thoughts that align with your goals for financial success.

Meditation can also serve as a powerful tool for addressing and overcoming financial fears. Many individuals harbor deep-seated anxieties about money that can hinder their progress toward wealth. During your meditation, focus on acknowledging these fears without judgment. Visualize them dissolving as you breathe deeply, allowing you to release the emotional weight they carry. This practice not only alleviates stress but also empowers you to approach financial situations with confidence and clarity.

Lastly, gratitude is a critical component in attracting wealth through your meditation practice. Cultivating a sense of gratitude for what you currently have opens the door for more abundance to flow into your life. Dedicate a portion of your meditation to reflecting on the blessings in your life, whether they are financial or otherwise. By establishing daily habits and rituals centered around gratitude, you reinforce a mindset that recognizes and attracts wealth, setting the stage for a successful financial future.

Chapter 6: The Role of Gratitude in Attracting Wealth

How Gratitude Affects Mindset

Gratitude plays a profound role in shaping our mindset, particularly when it comes to financial success. It is a powerful emotional state that can reprogram our subconscious, fostering a positive outlook on wealth and abundance. When we cultivate gratitude, we shift our focus from scarcity to abundance, allowing us to see opportunities for financial growth that we might otherwise overlook. This shift not only alters our perception but also influences our actions, enabling us to make decisions that align with our newfound mindset.

Engaging in daily gratitude practices can significantly enhance our ability to visualize wealth and attract it into our lives. By acknowledging the good that already exists, we set a foundation of positivity that enhances our visualization techniques. For instance, when we visualize our financial goals, the clarity and intensity of our vision can be amplified by the energy of gratitude. This combination creates a magnetic effect, drawing more wealth and opportunities toward us. As we express gratitude for what we have and what we aim to achieve, our subconscious becomes more receptive to the belief that financial abundance is not just possible but inevitable.

Affirmations serve as another vital tool in reprogramming our subconscious for financial success, and gratitude can significantly enhance their effectiveness. When we incorporate expressions of gratitude into our affirmations, we create a powerful synergy that reinforces our intentions. For example, affirming, "I am grateful for the wealth I attract every day," not only affirms our desire for financial abundance but also acknowledges the wealth that is already present in our lives. This practice fosters a sense of fulfillment, making it easier to believe in our potential to achieve financial freedom.

Meditation strategies can also be enriched by the practice of gratitude. By meditating on the things we are thankful for, we can quiet our minds and overcome financial fears that often hold us back. During meditation, focusing on gratitude allows us to cultivate a sense of peace and abundance, which can dissolve feelings of anxiety related to money. This state of mind is conducive to developing resilience against financial stressors, equipping us with a more robust mindset to face challenges and seize opportunities in our financial journeys.

Creating a wealth mindset through daily habits and rituals is essential for long-term financial success, and gratitude should be at the core of these practices. Establishing a routine that incorporates moments of gratitude can transform our approach to money and wealth. Simple actions, such as writing down three things we are grateful for each day or reflecting on past financial successes, can reinforce a positive mindset. Over time, these habits will not only change our perspective but also attract more abundance into our lives, ultimately leading us to a state of financial freedom.

Daily Gratitude Practices

Daily gratitude practices serve as a powerful tool for reprogramming the subconscious mind, particularly in the context of attracting financial abundance. When individuals consciously express gratitude, they shift their focus from scarcity to abundance, fostering a mindset that aligns with wealth attraction. This shift is crucial because the subconscious mind responds to the beliefs and emotions that dominate our conscious thoughts. By regularly acknowledging the positive aspects of our financial situation—no matter how small—individuals can cultivate an attitude of appreciation that opens the door to greater prosperity.

Incorporating gratitude into daily routines can take many forms. One effective method is to maintain a gratitude journal dedicated to financial blessings. Each day, individuals can write down at least three things they are grateful for regarding their financial situation. This practice not only reinforces a positive outlook but also creates a record of abundance that can be revisited during challenging times. Over time, this ritual can help to retrain the subconscious mind, making it more receptive to opportunities for wealth creation. The act of writing also solidifies these thoughts, making them more tangible and impactful.

Visualization practices can be enhanced through gratitude by incorporating feelings of thankfulness into the imagery. When visualizing financial goals, individuals can imagine not only achieving those goals but also feeling gratitude for them. This practice aligns emotions with intentions, making the visualization process more potent. By vividly imagining the experience of receiving wealth and expressing gratitude for it, the subconscious mind begins to accept this scenario as a reality, thus attracting similar experiences into one's life. Combining visualization with gratitude creates a powerful synergy that amplifies the effectiveness of both practices.

Affirmations related to wealth can also be infused with gratitude to further reinforce positive beliefs about financial success. For instance, instead of simply affirming "I am wealthy," individuals can say, "I am grateful for the wealth that flows into my life." This simple adjustment adds depth and emotional resonance to the affirmation, making it more effective. By acknowledging gratitude in affirmations, individuals signal to their subconscious that they not only seek wealth but also recognize and appreciate its presence, fostering a deeper sense of abundance.

Meditation is another powerful vehicle for cultivating gratitude, especially in overcoming financial fears. Setting aside time for daily meditation allows individuals to center themselves and reflect on their financial journey. During these sessions, focusing on what one is grateful for can help to alleviate anxieties about money. By fostering a sense of calm and appreciation, individuals can reframe their relationship with money and reduce feelings of fear and scarcity. Ultimately, these daily gratitude practices not only enhance overall well-being but also play a crucial role in creating a wealth mindset, fostering habits and rituals that attract financial success.

Transforming Your Financial Reality through Gratitude

Transforming your financial reality through gratitude begins with the understanding that your mindset plays a crucial role in how you perceive and interact with wealth. Gratitude is not merely a passive feeling; it is an active, conscious choice that can reshape your financial experiences. By acknowledging and appreciating what you already have, you create a fertile ground for attracting more abundance into your life. This shift in perspective allows you to move away from scarcity thinking, which often breeds fear and anxiety, toward a mindset that recognizes opportunities and potential.

Daily gratitude practices can significantly enhance your ability to attract wealth. When you consistently express gratitude for your current financial situation, no matter how modest, you signal to your subconscious mind that you are open to receiving more. This practice can take many forms, such as keeping a gratitude journal where you note down the positive aspects of your financial life or verbally expressing thanks for the resources you do possess. These rituals help cultivate a wealth mindset, reinforcing the belief that you are deserving of abundance and that prosperity is within your reach.

Visualization, when paired with gratitude, can be a powerful tool for manifesting financial success. Picture yourself living in a state of abundance, fully aware of the blessings you already have. As you visualize your financial goals, infuse those images with feelings of gratitude. This combination can program your subconscious mind to align with your conscious aspirations. The more vividly you can see yourself achieving financial freedom while feeling grateful for your journey, the more likely you are to attract those experiences into your reality.

Meditation is another effective strategy for overcoming financial fears and enhancing your gratitude practice. By creating a quiet space for reflection, you can explore and release limiting beliefs around money. As you meditate, focus on the feelings of gratitude that arise when you think about your financial achievements, no matter how small. This practice not only calms your mind but also reinforces a positive relationship with money. As you clear away fear and anxiety, you make room for new opportunities and insights that can lead to financial growth.

Incorporating gratitude into your daily habits and rituals can lead to profound changes in your financial reality. Make it a point to celebrate small wins, whether it's paying off a debt, finding a bargain, or simply having enough to meet your needs. This recognition fuels a positive feedback loop that encourages you to continue pursuing financial goals. By consistently practicing gratitude, you not only transform your mindset but also reprogram your subconscious to embrace abundance, ultimately paving the way for lasting financial success.

Chapter 7: Creating a Wealth Mindset through Daily Habits

Identifying Limiting Beliefs

Identifying limiting beliefs is a crucial step in the journey toward financial success and abundance. These beliefs, often deeply ingrained in our subconscious, can create barriers to achieving the wealth we desire. Limiting beliefs are thoughts that constrain our potential and hinder our ability to take action. They can stem from personal experiences, societal conditioning, or inherited family beliefs about money. Recognizing these beliefs is essential because they often dictate our financial behaviors and decisions, leading us to subconsciously sabotage our own efforts to achieve financial freedom.

One effective method for identifying limiting beliefs is through self-reflection. Take time to examine your thoughts and feelings surrounding money. Ask yourself questions such as: What beliefs do I hold about wealth? Do I think money is inherently wrong or difficult to obtain? Often, the answers to these questions reveal the subconscious narratives that influence our financial reality. Journaling can be an invaluable tool in this process, allowing you to articulate these beliefs and confront them directly. By bringing these beliefs into the light of consciousness, you pave the way for transformation.

Visualization practices can also aid in uncovering limiting beliefs. Visualize the life you desire and the financial abundance you wish to attract. As you engage in this practice, pay attention to any opposing thoughts or feelings that arise. These reactions can provide insight into the underlying beliefs that may be holding you back. For instance, if you visualize a prosperous life and feel anxious or unworthy, it indicates a limiting belief that you must address. By identifying these emotional triggers, you can begin the work of reprogramming your subconscious mind to align with your wealth goals.

Affirmations play a significant role in reshaping limiting beliefs. Once you have identified specific beliefs that restrict your financial growth, you can create positive affirmations that challenge and replace these thoughts. For instance, if you recognize a belief that "I will never be wealthy," you can affirm, "I am open to receiving abundant wealth." Repeating these affirmations consistently helps to rewire your subconscious, gradually diminishing the power of limiting beliefs. This practice, combined with daily rituals focused on gratitude for what you already have, reinforces a mindset conducive to attracting wealth.

Finally, meditation strategies can be beneficial in overcoming financial fears that often stem from limiting beliefs. Regular meditation allows you to quiet the mind and observe your thoughts without judgment. During these sessions, focus on releasing fear and doubt associated with money. By cultivating awareness of these fears, you can confront and dismantle the limiting beliefs tied to them. Integrating gratitude into your meditation practice further enhances this process, as it shifts your focus from scarcity to abundance. This comprehensive approach fosters a wealth mindset that supports your journey toward financial freedom.

Daily Habits for Financial Success

Daily habits play a crucial role in shaping our mindset and behaviors toward financial success. Establishing routines that promote positive thinking and reinforce the belief in our ability to achieve wealth is essential. By consciously integrating these practices into our daily lives, we not only enhance our awareness of financial opportunities but also reprogram our subconscious mind to align with our wealth goals. This can be achieved through consistent visualization, affirmations, meditation, and gratitude practices, each contributing to a stronger financial mindset.

Visualization is a powerful tool for attracting wealth. By spending a few minutes each day imagining your financial goals, you create a clear mental image of what success looks like. This practice not only helps clarify your objectives but also sends a strong message to your subconscious, encouraging it to seek opportunities that align with your visualized outcomes. To maximize the effectiveness of visualization, find a quiet space, close your eyes, and vividly envision your life as if you have already achieved your financial goals. Engage all your senses in this exercise, and allow yourself to feel the emotions associated with your success.

Affirmations are another key component of reprogramming your subconscious for financial success. By repeating positive statements about your financial abilities and worthiness, you can gradually shift your mindset from scarcity to abundance. Incorporate affirmations such as "I am deserving of financial prosperity" or "Money flows easily into my life" into your daily routine. Speaking these affirmations aloud, writing them down, or even recording them and listening to them can reinforce their impact. Over time, these affirmations will help dismantle limiting beliefs and replace them with a more empowering narrative about money.

Meditation is an essential practice for overcoming financial fears and anxieties. By dedicating time each day to quiet your mind and focus on your breath, you create a space for reflection and clarity. During meditation, you can acknowledge any financial fears that arise and visualize releasing them. This practice not only reduces stress but also enhances your ability to approach financial matters with a calm and open mindset. Additionally, meditation can serve as a moment to connect with your deeper desires, allowing you to align your actions with your financial aspirations.

Gratitude is a fundamental principle in attracting wealth. Cultivating a daily gratitude practice helps shift your focus from what you lack to appreciating what you already have. Each day, take a moment to reflect on the financial blessings in your life, no matter how small. This could include a steady income, supportive relationships, or lessons learned from past financial mistakes. By acknowledging these aspects, you create a positive energy that attracts more abundance into your life. Consistently expressing gratitude strengthens your wealth mindset, making it easier to recognize and seize new financial opportunities as they arise.

Rituals to Reinforce a Wealth Mindset

Rituals to reinforce a wealth mindset are essential tools for anyone striving to achieve financial freedom. These practices help to reshape our subconscious beliefs about money, instilling a sense of abundance rather than scarcity. By incorporating specific rituals into daily routines, individuals can gradually shift their mindset, making it easier to attract wealth and opportunities. The key lies in consistency and intention, as these rituals serve as a foundation upon which a prosperous mindset can be built.

Visualization practices are a powerful method for manifesting financial success. Taking time each day to envision oneself achieving financial goals can create a strong emotional connection to those aspirations. This practice involves finding a quiet space, closing the eyes, and picturing oneself living a life of abundance. Imagining the feelings associated with financial freedom, such as joy, security, and fulfillment, reinforces the belief that these goals are attainable. Over time, this visualization becomes a catalyst for action, encouraging individuals to pursue opportunities that align with their newfound mindset.

Affirmations serve as another vital component in the journey toward financial empowerment. By repeating positive statements related to wealth and abundance, individuals can reprogram their subconscious minds. Simple affirmations such as "I attract wealth effortlessly" or "I am deserving of financial success" can be powerful when spoken daily. Writing these affirmations down and placing them where they can be seen regularly further strengthens their impact.

This practice cultivates a sense of self-worth and confidence, making it easier to recognize and seize financial opportunities.

Meditation strategies play a crucial role in overcoming financial fears that may hinder progress. Engaging in regular meditation helps calm the mind and allows individuals to confront their anxieties about money. By focusing on the breath and observing thoughts without judgment, one can create a space for reflection and growth. This practice promotes emotional resilience and clarity, enabling individuals to approach financial challenges with a more balanced perspective. Ultimately, meditation fosters a sense of peace, making it easier to align with a wealth mindset.

Gratitude is a transformative ritual that can significantly enhance one's ability to attract wealth. Taking time each day to acknowledge and appreciate what one already has lays the groundwork for abundance. Keeping a gratitude journal, where individuals list things they are thankful for, can shift focus from lack to abundance. This simple act cultivates a positive outlook, reinforcing the belief that there is always enough. Moreover, expressing gratitude for future financial successes can amplify the law of attraction, drawing even more wealth into one's life. By incorporating these rituals into daily habits, anyone can create a sustainable wealth mindset rooted in abundance and possibility.

Chapter 8: Building a Supportive Environment

Surrounding Yourself with Positive Influences

Surrounding yourself with positive influences is an essential aspect of cultivating a mindset conducive to financial success. The people we interact with, the environments we inhabit, and the media we consume all play significant roles in shaping our beliefs and attitudes toward wealth. When you consciously choose to surround yourself with individuals who embody a positive attitude toward money and success, you create an atmosphere that encourages growth and abundance. This environment not only supports your financial aspirations but also reinforces the subconscious programming you are working to establish.

One effective way to ensure that positive influences surround you is to actively engage with a community that shares your goals and values. This could be a group of like-minded individuals who are also focused on achieving financial independence or mentors who have successfully navigated the journey you aspire to take. By surrounding yourself with those who inspire and uplift you, you create a network of support that encourages you to stay committed to your financial goals. Additionally, this community can provide valuable insights and strategies that can further enhance your wealth-building efforts.

Furthermore, the media and information you consume play a crucial role in shaping your beliefs about wealth and success.

It is vital to curate your media intake to include resources that promote positive financial mindsets, such as books, podcasts, and online courses focused on wealth attraction and financial literacy. By immersing yourself in content that reinforces your goals and aspirations, you reinforce the affirmations and visualizations you practice. This strategic approach to information consumption helps to reprogram your subconscious mind, aligning it with your conscious desire for financial abundance.

Gratitude is another powerful tool in attracting wealth, and the influences around you can significantly impact your ability to cultivate a grateful mindset. Engaging with individuals who practice gratitude and acknowledge their successes can inspire you to do the same. Regularly expressing gratitude for what you have, as well as for the financial opportunities that come your way, shifts your focus from lack to abundance. This shift not only enhances your emotional well-being but also opens the door for more wealth to flow into your life as you become a magnet for positive experiences.

Lastly, creating a wealth mindset through daily habits and rituals is greatly enhanced by positive influences. Establishing routines that promote mindfulness, such as meditation and visualization, can be more effective when practiced within a supportive environment. Engage with practices that encourage collective growth, such as group meditations or affirmation sessions. By incorporating these rituals into your daily life while surrounded by positivity, you solidify your commitment to financial freedom and establish a lifestyle that reflects your aspirations. In this way, the influences you choose to embrace become a powerful catalyst for your journey toward affirmative wealth.

The Importance of Community

Community plays a pivotal role in the journey toward financial success and personal growth. When individuals seek to reprogram their subconscious minds for wealth, they often overlook the profound impact that a supportive community can have. Communities provide networks of encouragement, shared experiences, and collective wisdom, which can significantly enhance one's ability to visualize and attract wealth. Engaging with like-minded individuals allows for the exchange of ideas and strategies, which can lead to deeper insights and a greater understanding of wealth creation.

Visualization practices are greatly enriched within a community setting. When individuals come together to share their visions for financial success, they create a collective energy that amplifies the manifestation process. Group visualization sessions can foster an environment of accountability and motivation, encouraging each member to stay committed to their goals. This shared focus not only strengthens individual resolve but also enhances the vibrational frequency of wealth attraction as members support one another in their endeavors and celebrate each other's successes.

Affirmations for subconscious programming are another area where community can be incredibly beneficial. When affirmations are spoken aloud in a group, they hold a powerful resonance that can penetrate deeper into the subconscious. Positive reinforcement from peers can bolster one's confidence in the affirmations being practiced. Moreover, hearing others affirm their financial intentions can inspire individuals to expand their own beliefs about what is possible, creating a ripple effect of abundance and positivity. This collective practice helps to dismantle limiting beliefs about money and fosters a more abundant mindset.

Meditation strategies that focus on overcoming financial fears can also be enhanced through community involvement. Group meditation sessions create a safe space where individuals can confront their fears around money in a supportive environment. Sharing experiences and insights with others allows for a greater understanding of everyday financial anxieties, helping members realize they are not alone in their struggles. This shared vulnerability can facilitate healing and lead to more profound transformations as members support each other in overcoming obstacles and nurturing a healthier relationship with money.

Finally, the role of gratitude in attracting wealth is significantly amplified in a community context. When individuals express gratitude collectively, the positive energy generated can be transformative. Regular gratitude practices within a community encourage members to recognize and celebrate not only their successes but also the abundance that exists in their lives. This fosters a culture of appreciation that reinforces the belief in the possibility of financial freedom. By creating daily habits and rituals centered around gratitude, community members can cultivate a wealth mindset that aligns with their financial goals, reinforcing the truth that together, they can achieve more than they ever could alone.

Creating a Wealth-Conducive Space

Creating a wealth-conducive space involves more than merely organizing your physical environment; it encompasses cultivating a mindset and atmosphere that supports financial abundance. This subchapter will explore the essential elements of this transformative process, emphasizing the interplay between your conscious thoughts and subconscious programming. By consciously designing your environment and mindset, you can lay the groundwork for attracting and sustaining wealth in your life.

To begin, consider the physical space around you. Your home and workplace should reflect abundance and positivity. This can be achieved through decluttering, as a tidy environment fosters clarity and focus. Surround yourself with items that inspire you, such as images of financial goals or symbols of success. Incorporate colors that evoke feelings of prosperity—greens, golds, and blues can all serve to elevate your mood and promote a sense of abundance. Additionally, ensuring that your space is well-lit and welcoming can significantly impact your mindset, encouraging you to engage in practices that align with your wealth goals.

Visualization practices play a critical role in creating a wealth-conducive space. By taking time each day to visualize your financial success, you engage both your conscious and subconscious mind in the manifestation process. Find a quiet area in your home where you can sit comfortably, close your eyes, and vividly picture your desired financial state. Imagine the sensations, emotions, and experiences associated with achieving your goals. This practice not only enhances your focus but also strengthens the neural pathways related to wealth creation, making it easier for your subconscious to align with your financial aspirations.

Affirmations serve as powerful tools to reinforce the wealth mindset you are developing. Craft specific affirmations that resonate with your financial goals and repeat them daily. Phrases such as "I am worthy of financial abundance" or "Wealth flows easily into my life" can help reprogram limiting beliefs and replace them with empowering thoughts. Incorporating these affirmations into your daily rituals—such as during meditation, while journaling, or even while commuting—can solidify your commitment to attracting wealth. The more consistently you affirm these beliefs, the more they will sink into your subconscious, shaping your actions and decisions regarding money.

Finally, cultivating gratitude is essential in creating a wealth-conducive space. Gratitude shifts your focus from scarcity to abundance, allowing you to appreciate what you already have while inviting more prosperity into your life. Establish a daily gratitude practice where you take a moment to acknowledge the financial blessings in your life, no matter how small. This could be as simple as being thankful for your current job, the opportunity to learn about financial success, or the support of friends and family. By integrating gratitude into your daily habits and rituals, you not only enhance your wealth mindset but also attract greater financial opportunities, creating a virtuous cycle of abundance.

Chapter 9: Tracking Progress and Celebrating Success

Measuring Your Financial Growth

Measuring your financial growth is an essential aspect of achieving and maintaining wealth. To effectively track your progress, you must first establish clear financial goals. These goals should be specific, measurable, achievable, relevant, and time-bound (SMART). For instance, instead of simply aiming to "save more money," you might set a goal to save $5,000 within the following year. By defining your objectives in this manner, you create a tangible target that will allow you to monitor your advancements. Regularly reviewing your goals and adjusting them as necessary will help you stay focused and motivated on your journey toward financial freedom.

Once you have established your financial goals, it is crucial to implement a reliable system for tracking your progress. Utilizing tools such as spreadsheets, budgeting apps, or financial journals can help you maintain a clear overview of your income, expenses, and savings. Recording your financial activities regularly fosters accountability and encourages positive financial habits. Additionally, this practice allows you to identify patterns in your spending and saving behaviors, enabling you to adjust your strategies as needed for optimal results.

Visualization practices can significantly enhance your ability to measure financial growth. By vividly imagining your desired financial outcomes, you can create a mental roadmap that guides your actions. Spend time each day visualizing not only the wealth you wish to attract but also the steps you need to take to achieve it. This mental exercise strengthens the connection between your conscious and subconscious mind, reinforcing your commitment to your financial goals. As you visualize your success, you may find it easier to recognize and seize opportunities that align with your aspirations.

Affirmations play a vital role in reprogramming your subconscious mind to support your financial growth. By consistently repeating positive statements related to money, such as "I am worthy of financial abundance" or "I attract wealth easily," you can shift your mindset from one of limitation to one of possibility. These affirmations can be integrated into your daily routine, perhaps during your morning meditation or while journaling. Over time, this practice will help solidify the belief that you can achieve your financial goals, making it easier to measure your growth in terms of both financial milestones and personal development.

Finally, cultivating a sense of gratitude is fundamental to attracting wealth and recognizing your financial growth. Regularly reflecting on what you are thankful for, including your financial achievements, fosters a positive mindset that supports abundance. Consider keeping a gratitude journal where you note down your financial victories, no matter how small they may seem. This practice not only reinforces your appreciation for what you have but also amplifies your awareness of your progress. By celebrating your accomplishments, you create a positive feedback loop that encourages further growth and abundance, leading to a more prosperous financial future.

Celebrating Milestones

Celebrating milestones is an essential practice in the journey toward financial freedom. Each step along the path to wealth, whether big or small, deserves recognition. Acknowledging these milestones not only reinforces your commitment but also serves as a powerful motivational tool. For individuals focused on reprogramming their subconscious minds, celebrating achievements—like reaching a savings goal, landing a new client, or completing a financial course—can create positive feedback loops that further encourage success. This practice helps embed the belief that you are capable of achieving your financial aspirations.

Visualization plays a crucial role in celebrating these milestones. When you take time to visualize your achievements, you enhance your subconscious programming. Picture yourself enjoying the benefits of your hard work—whether it's traveling to a destination you've always dreamt of or experiencing financial security. By creating vivid mental images of your accomplishments, you not only affirm your success but also condition your mind to seek out further opportunities that align with your wealth goals. This process of visualization reinforces the idea that financial success is not just possible but that it is an inevitable outcome of your efforts.

Affirmations are another powerful tool in this process. Crafting affirmations that celebrate your milestones can transform the way you perceive your financial journey. Instead of focusing solely on what you have yet to achieve, use affirmations to acknowledge your progress. Phrases like "I am proud of my financial achievements" or "Every step I take brings me closer to my goals" can shift your mindset. This shift is crucial in reprogramming your subconscious, allowing you to view your financial journey through a lens of abundance rather than scarcity.

Incorporating meditation strategies to reflect on your milestones can further enhance your wealth mindset. Setting aside time to meditate on your achievements allows you to connect deeply with the feelings of success and gratitude. During these moments of reflection, you can visualize the challenges you've overcome and the lessons learned along the way. This practice not only alleviates financial fears but also cultivates a sense of peace and confidence in your financial abilities. By regularly meditating on your progress, you solidify a mindset that is conducive to attracting even more wealth.

Finally, the role of gratitude in celebrating milestones cannot be overstated. Cultivating an attitude of gratitude creates an energetic alignment with abundance. When you express gratitude for your achievements, no matter how small, you acknowledge the effort and intention behind them. This practice encourages a wealth mindset, reinforcing the belief that you are deserving of financial success. By integrating gratitude into your daily habits and rituals, you create a fertile environment for attracting wealth and prosperity, ensuring that every milestone celebrated becomes a stepping stone toward your ultimate financial goals.

Adjusting Your Strategies for Continuous Improvement

Adjusting your strategies for continuous improvement is essential for anyone seeking financial freedom. The journey toward wealth is not a one-time event but a constant process of growth and development. As you delve into the principles of subconscious programming, it is crucial to regularly assess the effectiveness of your current strategies and make necessary adjustments. This proactive approach ensures that you remain aligned with your financial goals and are responsive to any changes in your circumstances or mindset.

One of the primary methods for adjusting your strategies is by utilizing visualization practices. Visualization helps you create a vivid mental image of your financial goals, allowing your subconscious mind to internalize these desires. To enhance your visualization techniques, consider incorporating specific details about your financial aspirations, such as the lifestyle you envision or the impact of wealth on your life. As you engage in this practice regularly, evaluate how your visualizations evolve and whether they still resonate with your true desires. Adjusting the imagery to reflect your growth and aspirations can lead to more effective subconscious programming.

Affirmations play a significant role in reprogramming your subconscious mind, particularly concerning financial success. To ensure that your affirmations remain relevant and impactful, revisit them periodically. Reflect on your progress and identify any limiting beliefs that may have surfaced. Adjust your affirmations to counteract these beliefs, focusing on empowering statements that resonate with your current journey. This practice not only reinforces your commitment to financial freedom but also enhances your ability to cultivate a wealth mindset by continuously affirming your potential.

Meditation strategies can also be refined to support your financial goals. As you meditate, take the time to explore any financial fears or anxieties that may arise. Acknowledging these fears can help you understand their origins and diminish their hold on your mindset. As you progress, adapt your meditation practices to incorporate techniques specifically designed to overcome these fears, such as guided visualizations or breathwork focused on abundance. The adjustments you make in your meditation practice can lead to deeper insights and a more profound transformation of your financial mindset.

Lastly, the role of gratitude in attracting wealth cannot be overstated. Regularly practicing gratitude helps shift your focus from scarcity to abundance, which is essential for cultivating a wealth mindset. To ensure that your gratitude practice remains effective, consider adjusting the ways you express gratitude. This could involve journaling about your financial achievements, acknowledging the support you receive from others, or reflecting on the lessons learned from financial challenges. By diversifying your gratitude practices, you can maintain a solid connection to your financial goals and continue to attract opportunities for prosperity.

Embracing a mindset of continuous improvement in these areas will empower you to navigate your financial journey with resilience and optimism.

Chapter 10: Sustaining Financial Freedom

Maintaining a Wealth Mindset Long-Term

Maintaining a wealth mindset long-term requires a commitment to continuous growth and self-awareness. It is essential to understand that a wealth mindset is not a one-time achievement but rather a lifelong journey. By consciously programming your subconscious mind, you can cultivate habits and beliefs that foster financial success. This process begins with a clear understanding of your current beliefs about money and wealth, as well as the potential barriers that may hinder your financial progress. Regular self-reflection and assessment will help you identify areas that need improvement, allowing you to take proactive steps toward a more prosperous mindset.

Visualization practices play a crucial role in maintaining a wealth mindset. By vividly imagining your financial goals and the lifestyle you desire, you reinforce your commitment to achieving these aspirations. Visualization helps create a mental blueprint that guides your daily actions and decisions. To make this practice effective, set aside time each day to visualize your financial success. Picture yourself living in abundance, experiencing the freedom that comes from financial independence. This daily ritual not only strengthens your resolve but also aligns your subconscious mind with your conscious goals, making them more attainable.

Affirmations are another powerful tool for reprogramming your subconscious and sustaining a wealth mindset. By consistently repeating positive statements related to money and abundance, you can challenge and replace limiting beliefs. Choose affirmations that resonate with you and reflect your financial aspirations. For instance, affirming statements like "I am worthy of financial abundance" or "Money flows easily into my life" can shift your mindset towards one of receptivity and gratitude. Incorporate these affirmations into your daily routine, perhaps during your morning meditation or as part of your evening reflection, to reinforce a positive attitude towards wealth.

Meditation strategies are essential for overcoming financial fears that may arise in your journey towards wealth. By incorporating mindfulness and meditation into your daily life, you can cultivate a sense of calm and clarity that empowers you to tackle financial challenges. Begin with short meditation sessions focusing on your breath and allowing thoughts about money to surface without judgment. As you gain greater awareness of these thoughts, you can address and transform any fears or anxieties into opportunities for growth. This practice not only helps alleviate stress but also strengthens your resolve to maintain a wealth mindset in the face of adversity.

Lastly, the role of gratitude in attracting wealth cannot be overstated. Developing a gratitude practice allows you to shift your focus from scarcity to abundance. By regularly acknowledging and appreciating what you already have, you create a mindset that welcomes more prosperity into your life. Consider keeping a gratitude journal where you list things you are thankful for, particularly in relation to your financial situation. This simple yet powerful habit reinforces positive thinking and opens the door for further financial opportunities. By integrating gratitude into your daily rituals, you create a fertile ground for a sustainable wealth mindset that thrives over time.

Evolving Your Practices with Time

Evolving your practices with time is essential for personal growth, particularly in the realm of financial success. As you embark on your journey towards reprogramming your subconscious mind for wealth, it is necessary to recognize that the techniques and strategies that resonate with you may shift as your understanding deepens and your circumstances change. By being adaptable and open to new practices, you create a dynamic approach that can enhance your ability to attract financial abundance. This evolution can involve refining your visualization techniques, updating your affirmations, or even exploring new meditation practices that address your evolving financial fears.

Visualization practices are foundational in attracting wealth. Initially, you may start with simple visualizations of your financial goals. However, as you become more experienced, you can expand these visualizations to include detailed scenarios of your life with financial freedom. Consider incorporating sensory details—what you see, hear, and feel in these moments of success. This enhanced clarity not only strengthens your emotional connection to your goals but also makes your visualizations more powerful, ultimately aligning your subconscious with your conscious desires.

Affirmations play a crucial role in subconscious programming, and as you progress, it is beneficial to revisit and revise them regularly. Start with broad statements about wealth and abundance, but as you grow more confident, tailor your affirmations to specific goals and experiences. For example, instead of saying, "I am wealthy," you might say, "I am attracting multiple streams of income that support my lifestyle." This evolution in your affirmations helps to maintain their relevance and potency, ensuring that they continue to resonate with your current aspirations and mindset.

Meditation strategies can also evolve as you confront and overcome financial fears. Initially, you may focus on calming anxiety and building resilience. As you become more adept, consider integrating visualization techniques into your meditation sessions. Picture yourself successfully navigating financial challenges or embodying the traits of financially successful individuals. This integration creates a more holistic approach to your practice, allowing you to dismantle fears while simultaneously reinforcing a positive financial identity.

Finally, cultivating a gratitude practice is vital in attracting wealth, and its evolution can significantly impact your financial mindset. Begin by acknowledging small blessings in your life, but as your practice deepens, expand your gratitude to include financial aspects. Regularly express appreciation for your income, your skills, and the opportunities that come your way. This shift in focus not only enhances your overall well-being but also reinforces a wealth mindset that attracts more abundance. By continually evolving your practices, you create a foundation for lasting financial success that aligns with your personal growth and aspirations.

Inspiring Others on Their Financial Journeys

Inspiring others on their financial journeys begins with an understanding of the profound impact that mindset has on financial success. Each individual holds the power to reshape their financial reality through conscious thought and deliberate action. By embracing principles such as visualization, affirmations, and gratitude, we can not only transform our own lives but also motivate those around us to embark on their paths toward financial freedom. Encouraging a shift in perspective can ignite the spark of possibility within others, enabling them to see wealth not just as a destination but as a journey filled with growth and opportunity.

Visualization practices are a powerful tool for attracting wealth and abundance. When individuals can vividly imagine their financial goals—whether it's owning a home, starting a business, or achieving a certain level of savings—they create a mental blueprint for success. Sharing stories of triumph, where visualization played a crucial role, can inspire others to incorporate similar practices into their daily routines. By guiding them through the process of creating vision boards or engaging in visualization exercises, we can help them cultivate a clear and compelling vision of their financial future, making it easier to take actionable steps toward those dreams.

Affirmations serve as a vital component in programming the subconscious mind for financial success. By repeating positive statements about wealth and abundance, individuals can challenge and reframe limiting beliefs that may have been ingrained since childhood. Encouraging others to develop personalized affirmations can foster a sense of empowerment and agency over their financial situations. Sharing examples of effective affirmations and the transformative experiences of those who have adopted them can motivate individuals to take control of their financial narratives and instill a belief in their potential for prosperity.

Meditation strategies can be instrumental in overcoming financial fears and anxieties that often hinder progress. Many individuals carry deep-seated worries related to money, whether stemming from past experiences or societal conditioning. By introducing meditation techniques focused on financial abundance and security, we can help others cultivate a sense of calm and confidence in their financial decision-making. Group meditation sessions that focus on themes of wealth and abundance can create a supportive environment, allowing participants to connect with their intentions and visualize a future free from financial fear.

Gratitude plays an essential role in attracting wealth and fostering a positive wealth mindset. Encouraging individuals to adopt daily gratitude practices can shift their focus from scarcity to abundance. When people actively acknowledge and appreciate what they already have, they create space for more wealth to flow into their lives. Sharing stories of how gratitude has transformed financial situations can inspire others to integrate this practice into their daily rituals. By emphasizing the interconnectedness of gratitude, mindset, and financial success, we can empower others to cultivate a wealth mindset that is not only sustainable but also deeply fulfilling. It's a beautiful day.

Author Biography

Richard Trillion Mantey is a personal development expert and financial coach dedicated to helping individuals transform their relationships with money. With over 6 years of experience in psychology and finance, he specializes in empowering others to break free from limiting beliefs and cultivate a wealthy mindset. Richard Trillion Mantey combines practical strategies with deep psychological insights to guide readers toward financial freedom and abundance. Passionate about sharing knowledge, he has hosted workshops and seminars that inspire countless individuals to reprogram their subconscious minds for success. Richard Trillion Mantey lives in Burlington, Ontario, Canada, and enjoys Playing tennis, soccer, golf, and basketball with friends and family in Burlington, Ontario, Canada.

www.ingramcontent.com/pod-product-compliance
Lightning Source LLC
LaVergne TN
LVHW021544080426
835509LV00019B/2823